you will need

Each Sticky Little Fingers activity includes a list of all the things you will need. But here are some of the everyday things that will be useful for your rainy day crafts.

★

felt-tip pens

sheets of coloured paper

coloured card

stiff cardboard

crêpe paper

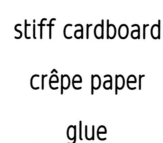

glue

pencil

assorted cardboard boxes

glitter

scraps of material

scraps of wool

string

paints

paintbrushes

sticky tape

needle and thread

scissors

pipe cleaners

white styrofoam balls

coloured pom-poms

coloured feathers

button magnets

paper fasteners

garden canes

plastic googly eyes

TAKE CARE!
Be very careful when you are cutting things out.
Never be afraid to ask a grown-up for help.

Money muncher

You will need

★ tall cardboard biscuit or crisp tube with a lid ★ scissors
★ sheets of coloured paper ★ glue ★ black felt-tip pen ★ pencil
★ pipe cleaners ★ white cotton balls ★ big and small pom-poms

What to do

1 Turn the tube upside down with the lid at the bottom and cover it with brightly coloured paper. Ask a grown-up to help you cut a coin-sized slit near the top. Then make a small hole on each side of the tube. for the pipe-cleaner arms.

2 Make two arms out of pipe cleaners. Bend each one in half and make three loops for hands. Twist the ends together, then glue the arms into the arm holes on the tube.

3 Glue on the white cotton balls for eyes and decorate the tube with pom-poms and letters cut from coloured paper. Wind pipe cleaners around pens to create springs and glue pom-poms to the ends. Tape the springs to the top of the money box.

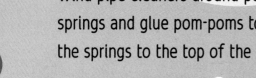

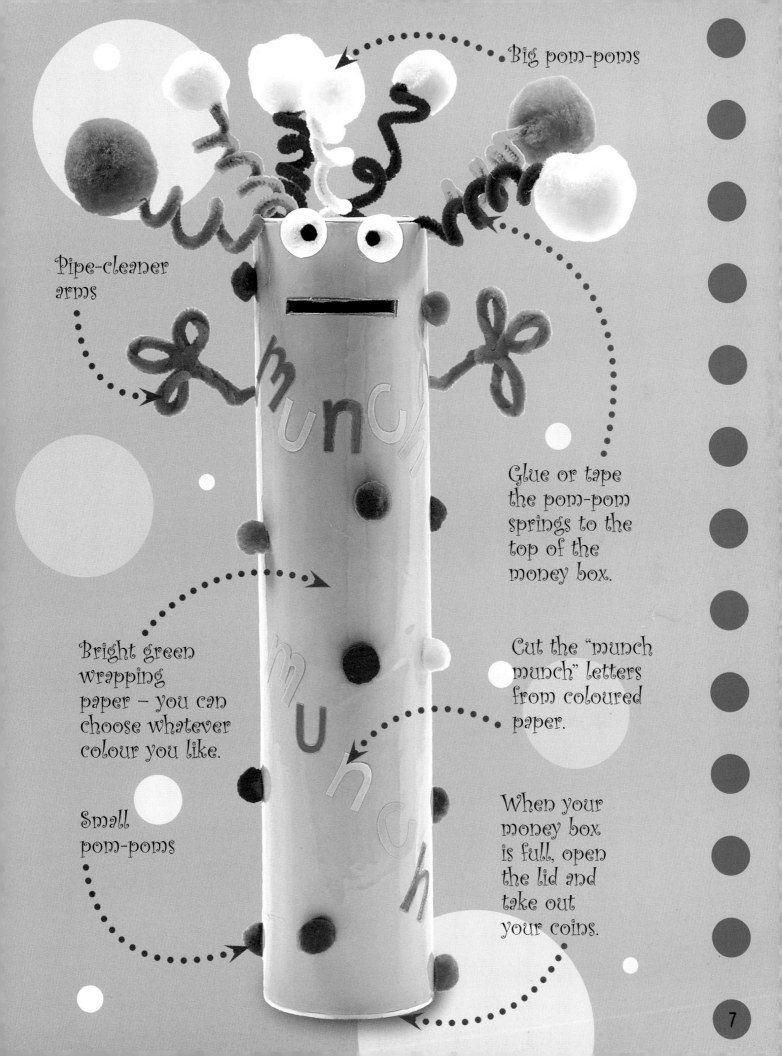

Big pom-poms

Pipe-cleaner arms

Glue or tape the pom-pom springs to the top of the money box.

Cut the "munch munch" letters from coloured paper.

Bright green wrapping paper – you can choose whatever colour you like.

When your money box is full, open the lid and take out your coins.

Small pom-poms

Celebration tree

You will need

★ twiggy branch ★ plant pot with one hole in the bottom
★ coloured card and paper ★ scissors ★ needle and thread
★ coloured feathers ★ plastic googly eyes ★ coloured ribbons and thread

What to do

1 Turn the plant pot upside down and put the thick end of your branch through the hole in the middle. If it wobbles, wrap sticky tape around the branch to make a tight fit.

2 Cut out shapes from coloured card and, using a needle, thread them onto cotton to make pretty garlands to decorate your tree.

3 To make birds, cut leaf shapes from coloured card and fold them lengthwise. Using a needle, sew on a loop of thread to hang them from your tree. Glue a colourful feather tail to one end and a googly eye to the other.

Try hanging up secret messages written on rolled-up strips of coloured paper.

Write greetings on coloured card shapes and hang them from the branches.

Happy Easter

Happy Birthday

Lengths of curling ribbon add colour to the branches.

Making a tree is a lovely way to celebrate any special occasion, such as a birthday, Easter, or a christening.

Pom-pom birds

You will need

★ cardboard pom-pom template ★ stiff cardboard ★ scissors
★ balls of coloured wool ★ black felt-tip pen ★ glue ★ coloured feathers
★ small white styrofoam balls ★ beak template ★ thick pipe cleaners

What to do

1 Cut out two cardboard rings using the template on page 48. Put the rings together and wind the wool around both until you can't push any more through the middle.

2 Using sharp scissors, ask a grown-up to help you cut through the wool around the edge of the ring. Tie a piece of wool tightly between the two cardboard rings, then remove the rings and fluff up your pom-pom.

3 Trim off any uneven ends from your pom-pom. Glue on the small white balls and add a dot to make eyes, then glue on the tail and wing feathers. Use the template on page 48 to make a cone-shaped beak from coloured card. Glue on the finished beak.

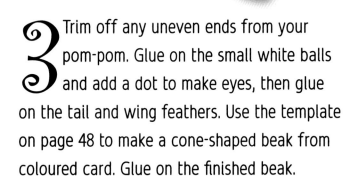

4 Make two feet out of pipe cleaners. Bend the pipe cleaner in half and make three loops for the foot, then twist the ends together to make the legs. Glue onto the pom-pom.

Brightly coloured feather tail ••••••

The thicker the wool, the quicker you will make the pom-pom.

Cardboard beak ••••••

Big feet make it easy for your bird to stand up.

11

Paper weaving

You will need

★ sheets of coloured paper or paper cut from a magazine
★ scissors ★ sticky tape ★ box ★ glue

What to do

1 Cut your pieces of paper into strips about 1 centimetre (¹/₂ inch wide). Make sure the strips are longer than the width of the box you want to cover.

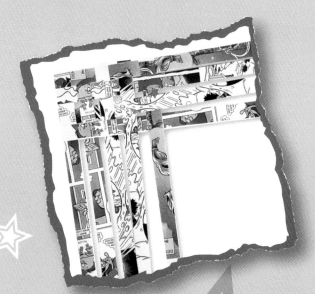

2 Lay a row of strips next to each other on your work top and stick them down with tape. Take some of the other strips and, one at a time, weave them over and under the strips you have stuck down to create a woven sheet.

3 When you have woven five panels, start to cover your box. Cut the panels to fit the sides of the box, allowing 1 centimetre (¹/₂ inch) at each side to wrap around corners. Glue them down. Paint the lid and glue a woven panel in the centre.

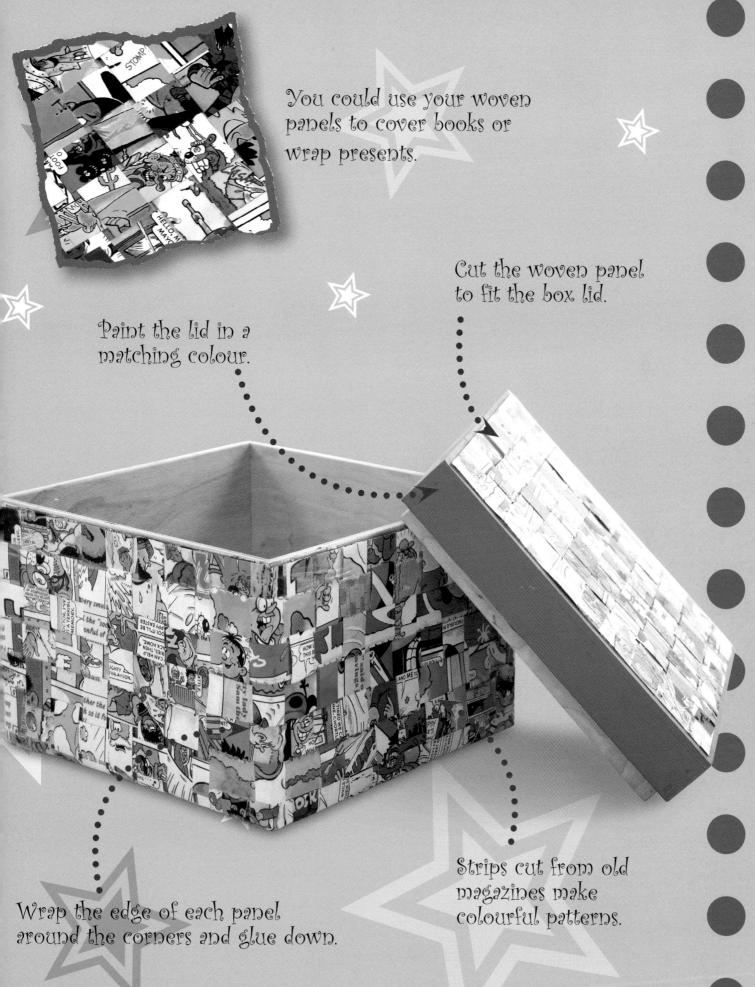

You could use your woven panels to cover books or wrap presents.

Cut the woven panel to fit the box lid.

Paint the lid in a matching colour.

Wrap the edge of each panel around the corners and glue down.

Strips cut from old magazines make colourful patterns.

Cheeky fridge magnets

You will need

★ 90 g (3 oz) plain white flour ★ 60 g (2 oz) salt
★ 2 teaspoons of cooking oil ★ water ★ acrylic or poster paints
★ bits of wool, string, or fabric ★ glue ★ button magnets

What to do

1 Mix together the flour, salt, oil, and enough water to make a firm salt dough. Knead the dough on a clean surface until smooth then divide it into three pieces. Break off lumps for the nose, ears, and eyes and use water to stick them onto the faces.

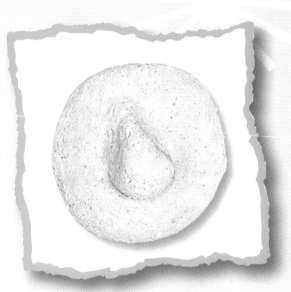

2 Leave the faces in a warm place to air-dry for a couple of days, or place them on a baking sheet in a low oven for about an hour, or until hard. Once they are dry, paint them. Add wool, string, fabric, or pipe cleaners for hair.

3 Once you have finished decorating your faces, turn them over and glue a button magnet onto the back of each one.

These eyes are made out of small balls of dough, but you could use plastic googly eyes.

This recipe makes three cheeky faces.

Snip pieces of fabric to make hair.

Scraps of wool

Shape the nose from the dough and glue it on with water.

15

Beans for tea!

You will need

★ quick-sprouting seeds such as alfalfa, mung beans, white radish
★ large, wide-mouthed glass jars ★ rubber bands
★ muslin or fine cloth to cover jar tops

What to do

1 Put 1 tablespoon of seeds into the jar. Fill halfway with cool water, then fasten a circle of muslin to the opening with a rubber band. Soak the seeds overnight. Drain the water from the jar through the muslin.

2 Rinse and drain the seeds twice a day to stop them from going bad. After about three days they will start to sprout. When the sprouts are 3 to 5 centimetres (1 to 2 inches) long, they're ready to eat.

3 If you want white shoots, leave your jar in a dark place. If you want green shoots, leave your jar in the light.

Try your sprouted seeds in a salad or a sandwich.

Blow-paint monsters

You will need

★ thick paper or card ★ paint ★ water ★ straw ★ felt-tip pens ★ plastic googly eyes

What to do

Googly eyes turn a splodge into a monster.

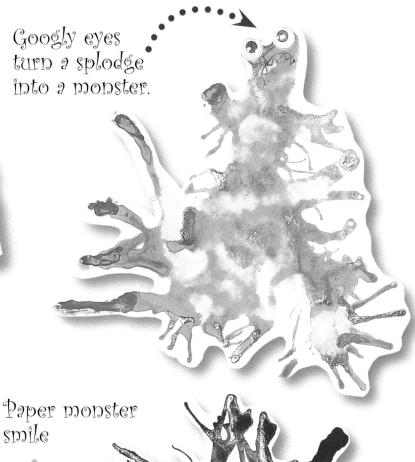

1 Apply a puddle of runny paint to your paper or card. Use a straw to blow the paint across the paper in different directions.

Paper monster smile

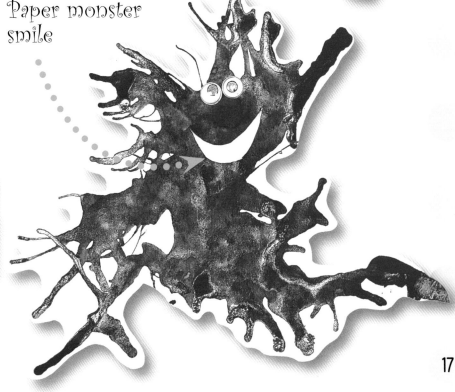

2 When the paint has dried you can add faces to create splodge monsters.

Teddy biscuits

You will need

★ 175 g (6 oz) butter ★ 100 g (3½ oz) caster sugar ★ egg yolk
★ 275 g (9½ oz) plain white flour ★ teddy biscuit template ★ cling film
★ rolling pin ★ knife ★ greased baking sheet ★ icing sugar ★ water
★ cocoa powder ★ coloured chocolate beans

What to do

1 Cream together the butter and caster sugar, then beat in an egg yolk. Sift in the flour and stir until it makes a dough. Wrap the dough in cling film and chill it in the fridge for 30 minutes before rolling out to about ½ centimetre (¼ inch) thick.

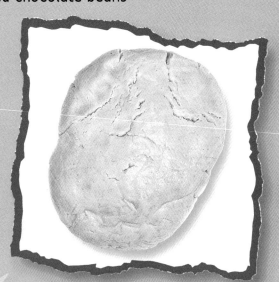

2 Using the template on page 48, cut out teddy shapes from the dough and place them on a greased baking sheet. Bake in the oven at 190°C (375°F/gas mark 5) for 10 minutes or until golden. Allow to cool.

3 Mix 8 tablespoons of icing sugar with enough water to make a thick paste. Divide the icing into two bowls and colour one brown by adding in 2 teaspoons of cocoa powder. Use the white icing to make the eyes and to glue on the chocolate-bean mouth. Use the brown icing for the nose.

Chocolate
icing-sugar
nose

Icing-sugar
eyes

Chocolate-bean
mouth

Puppet on a string

You will need

★ box ★ coloured paper ★ large styrofoam ball ★ small styrofoam ball
★ acrylic paint ★ sticky tape ★ glue ★ string ★ corrugated cardboard
★ plastic googly eyes ★ lengths of wool ★ buttons ★ glitter

What to do

1 Glue coloured paper and shapes to the box for the body, but leave the top and bottom open. Ask an adult to make two holes in the lid for the controls, and thread strings through the top and bottom of the box for the arms and legs.

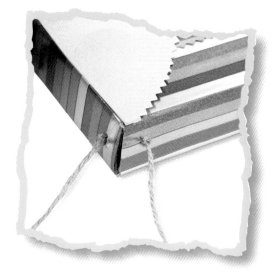

2 To make your puppet's controls, thread string through the holes in the lid of the box and tie a knot on the inside to fasten. Now close the top and bottom of the box and secure with tape. Tie the loose ends of string to a garden cane.

3 Paint the ball for the head and glue or tape it securely to the box. Glue on eyes, a nose, and a mouth. Make hair out of scraps of coloured wool.

4 Cut out two hands and two feet from corrugated cardboard. Ask an adult to make holes in them and knot them on to the ends of the arms and legs.

Googly eyes

Scraps of coloured wool

Painted ball nose

Cut out a mouth from coloured paper.

Add glitter to the body for an extra sparkle.

Stick on some buttons to make it look like real clothes.

Paint the hands.

Glue three or four layers of cardboard together to make extra chunky feet and hands.

Dickory dock clock

You will need

★ stiff cardboard ★ coloured card ★ scissors
★ templates for clock hands ★ paint ★ paper fastener
★ coloured paper ★ glue ★ cardboard box ★ templates for mouse
★ grey card ★ string ★ plastic googly eyes

What to do

1 Cut a large circle out of stiff cardboard 30 centimetres (12 inches) in diameter and paint it. Make a hole in the centre for the hands. Use the template on page 48 to cut out the two clock hands in coloured card. Make a hole in the non-pointed end of each hand.

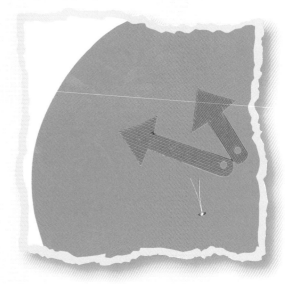

2 Fix the hands to the clock with a paper fastener. Cut numbers 1 to 12 out of coloured paper and glue them onto the face. If you like, you could glue the finished clock face onto a painted cardboard box.

3 To make the finger-puppet mouse use the templates on page 48. Cut a cone out of grey card for the body. Cut out and glue on the ears and googly eyes and add a length of string for a tail.

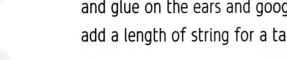

Move the hands around to practise telling the time.

Cut your numbers out of coloured paper.

Mouse's body is made from a cone of grey card.

Handprints and footprints

You will need

★ sheets of paper — all different sizes ★ liquid paint in lots of bright colours
★ shallow bowls or trays — big enough for feet ★ scissors ★ black felt-tip pen

What to do

1 Pour liquid paint into bowls — a separate bowl for each colour. Then dip in your hands and press them down onto the paper to create lots of fun pictures. Don't forget to wash your hands every time you change colour!

2 See how many different creatures you can make using handprints. When the paint is dry, cut out your handprints and glue them onto paper to make animals. Use a thick black pen to draw a face for your picture.

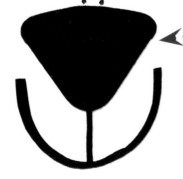

A thick black pen is great for making faces.

3 Now dip your bare feet into the paint and step onto a piece of paper to make prints. Try walking across a big piece of paper!

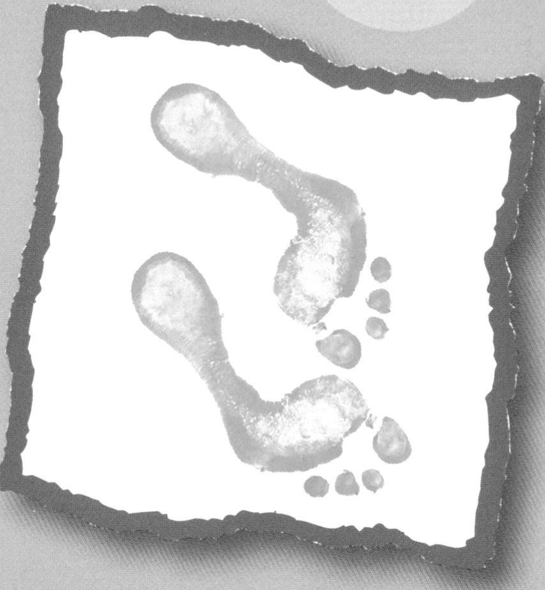

4 When your footprints are dry, cut them out and stick them on paper to make pictures of your favourite animals. You can also paint circles and other shapes to cut out and add to your picture.

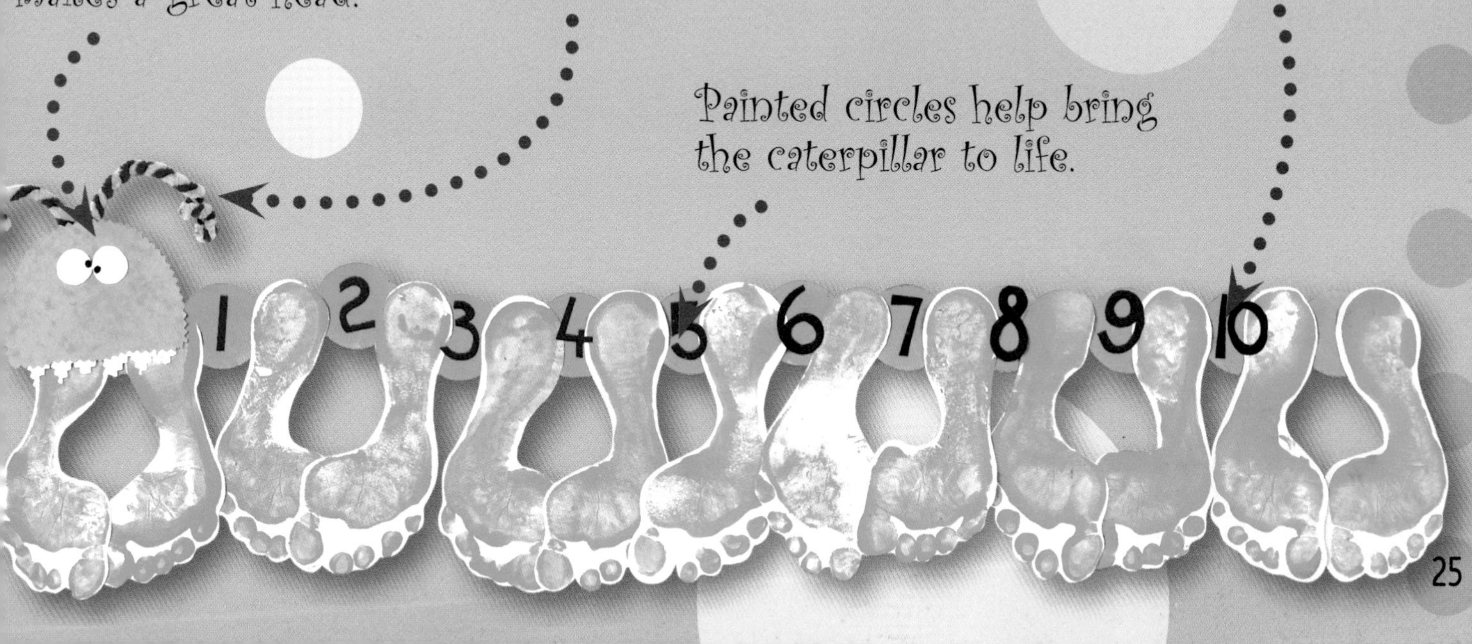

A painted semi-circle makes a great head.

Two twisted pipe cleaners make great antennae.

Numbers

Painted circles help bring the caterpillar to life.

1 2 3 4 5 6 7 8 9 10

Anyone for skittles?

You will need

★ 5 large cardboard biscuit or crisp tubes
★ 5 large sheets of coloured paper ★ scissors ★ glue
★ tennis ball to play the game

What to do

1 Collect five sturdy cardboard tubes. Cover them with coloured paper or paint them. Use a range of different colours. If you can't find enough cardboard tubes, you can make your skittles out of plastic drinks bottles.

2 Cut large numbers 1 to 5 out of coloured paper and glue one number on each skittle. Cut out lots of coloured shapes and glue them onto the skittles to decorate.

3 To play the game, line the skittles up, then, from a distance, take turns rolling a tennis ball at them to try to knock down as many as possible. The winner is the first to knock down all the skittles.

Cover each tube in coloured paper.

Cut big numbers out of coloured paper and glue on.

Cut out shapes from coloured paper.

Bright and breezy bunting

You will need

★ coloured paper ★ string or thread
★ scissors ★ sticky tape

What to do

1 Use a sharp pair of scissors and the template on page 48 to cut out lots of triangles of coloured paper.

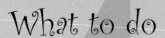

2 Decide how long you want your bunting to be and cut a length of string or thread. Space your triangles evenly along it and then fold the tops over the string and tape them securely.

3 When all your triangles are stuck down, your bunting is ready to hang. For a waterproof, outdoor bunting, cut triangles from coloured plastic bags. Colourful fabric triangles sewn onto tape will last for years.

Brighten up the dullest day with this jolly bunting, inside or out. It's great for birthdays and special occasions.

Pasta garland

You will need

★ tubular pasta ★ paint ★ string ★ cloth or ribbon

What to do

1 Place the tubular pasta in a bowl and pour runny paint over it. Stir well.

2 Once the pasta is coated with paint, transfer it to a non-stick baking tray and place it in the oven on a very low heat until it is dry, or leave it to dry in the air.

Thread the pasta onto the string.

Tie a loop in one end of a piece of string.

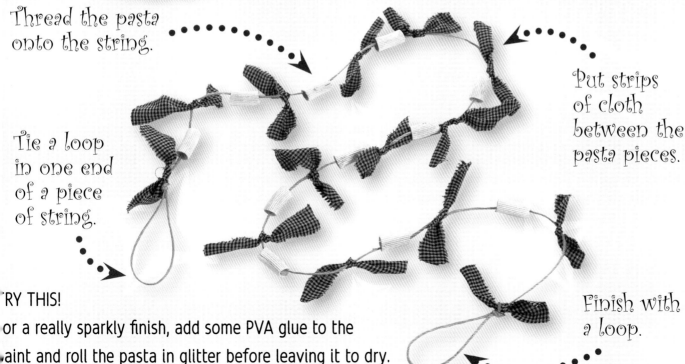

Put strips of cloth between the pasta pieces.

Finish with a loop.

TRY THIS!

For a really sparkly finish, add some PVA glue to the paint and roll the pasta in glitter before leaving it to dry.

Spooky spider cakes

You will need

★ packet of red sweetie sticks or laces ★ scissors
★ chocolate tea cakes ★ cocktail stick ★ icing sugar ★ water ★ sweetie eyes

What to do

1 Cut the sweetie sticks into 10-centimetre (4-inch) lengths to make the spider's legs. You will need eight legs for each spider.

2 Use a cocktail stick to pierce four small holes in the chocolate on each side of the tea cake. Carefully poke a leg into each hole.

3 Mix 4 tablespoons of icing sugar with a small amount of water to make a stiff paste and use it to glue the sweetie eyes onto the spiders. If you have extra sweets, you could add a nose and mouth, too.

Red
sweetie sticks

Use icing sugar to
glue on the eyes.

Chocolate
tea-cake body

Piñata pear

You will need

★ big balloon ★ sheets of old newspaper ★ PVA glue
★ small party toys ★ sweets ★ green crêpe paper

What to do

1 Choose the biggest balloon you can find and ask an adult to blow it up for you. Cut or tear up the sheets of newspaper into small strips.

2 Water down some PVA glue and cover the balloon with about five layers of paper, one layer at a time. Make sure you leave a hole somewhere that is large enough to poke your goodies through.

3 When the papier-mâché is dry, burst the balloon and fill the shape with toys and sweets. Cover the hole with paper, and when it is dry, decorate the piñata. We wound fringed crêpe paper strips around the balloon to make a pear and added paper leaves and a stem.

4 Ask an adult to thread some string through the top of the piñata and hang it high up, away from anything breakable. Take turns hitting the piñata with a stick. Eventually it will burst, and the goodies will be scattered around the room.

Decorate your piñata to make yours into a face or an animal.

A piñata is a fun way to end a party.

Fringed crêpe paper

To make the game last longer, children can be blindfolded and spun around, making it harder to hit the piñata.

Magnetic fishing game

You will need

★ template for fish ★ thick card ★ paint ★ strips of tin foil
★ glue ★ white paper ★ black felt-tip pen ★ metal paper clips
★ string ★ long stick ★ ring magnet

What to do

1 Using the template on page 48, cut out fish shapes from thick card and paint. When they are dry decorate each fish. We used scale-shaped strips of tin foil, but you could just as easily glue on glitter or coloured shapes.

2 Make the eyes by cutting out small circles from a piece of white paper. Add a dot in the middle and glue one eye on each fish.

3 Push a metal paper clip over the tip of the nose of each fish. Do not choose plastic-coated paper clips, as these will not be picked up by the magnet.

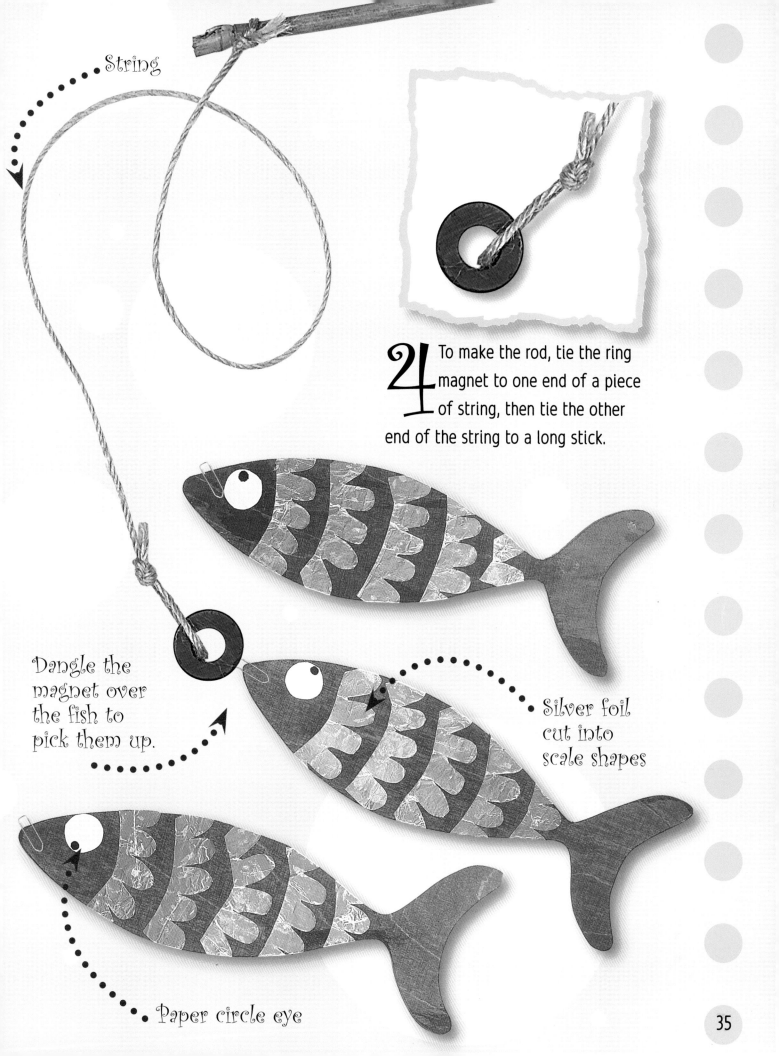

String

4 To make the rod, tie the ring magnet to one end of a piece of string, then tie the other end of the string to a long stick.

Dangle the magnet over the fish to pick them up.

Silver foil cut into scale shapes

Paper circle eye

ping-pong snake

You will need

★ 12 ping-pong balls ★ paint ★ string ★ scissors ★ coloured felt
★ coloured spot stickers ★ glue ★ big plastic googly eyes ★ small styrofoam balls

What to do

1 Ask an adult to make holes in the top and bottom of each ping-pong ball. Cut out 12 small felt triangles.

2 Paint the ping-pong balls. When they are dry, thread them all onto a piece of string and tie a knot at each end. Glue on the coloured felt triangles and decorate with sticky coloured spots.

3 Make a face at one end of your snake and decorate with googly eyes glued onto small, white styrofoam balls. The string looks just like a tongue.

Felt or foam shapes make great decoration.

Googly eyes

You could paint your snake lots of different colours.

Sticky coloured spots

A knot holds your snake together.

Gingerbread hearts

You will need

★ 180 g (6 oz) plain flour ★ 1 teaspoon bicarbonate of soda
★ 1 teaspoon ground ginger ★ 1 teaspoon ground cinnamon ★ 90 g (3 oz) caster sugar
★ 60 g (2 oz) butter, cut into pieces ★ 2 tablespoons of golden syrup
★ 1 beaten egg yolk ★ 1 heart-shaped cookie cutter ★ ribbon to thread

What to do

1 Sift together the flour, bicarbonate of soda, and spices. Rub the butter into the flour until the mixture resembles fine breadcrumbs. Alternatively you can do this in a food processor. Add the sugar, syrup, and egg yolk and mix to a firm dough. Form the dough into a ball and chill it in the fridge.

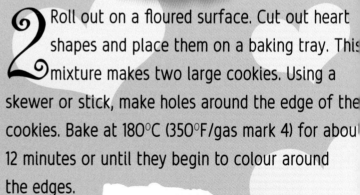

2 Roll out on a floured surface. Cut out heart shapes and place them on a baking tray. This mixture makes two large cookies. Using a skewer or stick, make holes around the edge of the cookies. Bake at 180°C (350°F/gas mark 4) for about 12 minutes or until they begin to colour around the edges.

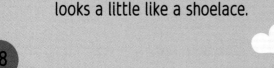

3 When the biscuits come out of the oven, re-form the holes with the skewer. Once the gingerbread hearts have cooled, thread with ribbon. To make the ribbon easier to thread, wrap a piece of tape tightly around one end, so that it looks a little like a shoelace.

Make sure the holes are not too close to the edge.

Tie the ribbon in a bow.

Shape race

You will need

★ stiff white card ★ coloured felt ★ scissors ★ 6 medium-sized pebbles
★ acrylic paints in 6 different colours ★ cube-shaped cardboard box

What to do

1 Cut out six squares of stiff white card and paint each one a different colour. You can decorate the edges with patterns if you wish. Mark one square with "start" and another with "finish".

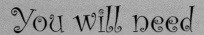

2 Paint the top of each pebble with white paint. While the paint is drying, cut out two squares, circles, triangles, diamonds, rectangles, and stars from the coloured felt. Use a different colour for each shape. Glue a different shape to the top of each pebble.

3 To make a dice, paint the box or cover it with coloured paper. Glue one of each of the pebble shapes onto each face of the dice.

start

Paint each square a different colour.

Glue a different felt shape to each side of the dice.

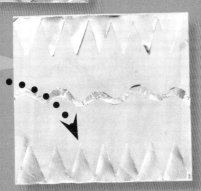

Decorate your squares with patterns and shapes.

Paint each pebble and glue a shape to the top.

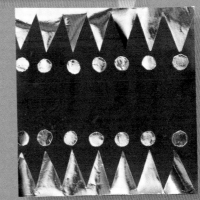

How to play

This is a game for up to six players

★ Place the coloured squares on the floor. Put the "start" square first and the "finish" square last.

★ Each player chooses a shape pebble and takes turns throwing the dice.

★ If the dice lands on your shape, you can move your pebble forward to the next square.

★ The first player to reach the finish line is the winner.

finish

Meringue monsters

You will need

★ 3 large egg whites ★ 175 g (6 oz) caster sugar ★ hand whisk ★ fromage frais
★ strawberry laces ★ cake decorations ★ sweets

What to do

1 Preheat the oven to 110°C (225°F/gas mark ½) and line a baking sheet with non-stick parchment paper. Beat the egg whites to form stiff peaks. Whisk in the sugar a little at a time, then spoon blobs of mixture onto the baking sheet. Bake for 2 hours.

2 When the meringues are cool, you can build them into monsters. Use fromage frais to stick them together. Make spooky arms out of strawberry laces, with knots for fingers at each end. Wrap the arms around your monster's neck.

3 Give your monsters scary faces using bright cake decorations or sweets for eyes. Stick the sweets on with a big blob of fromage frais.

Eyes made from cake decorations.

To colour your monsters, add a few drops of food colouring to the stiff egg whites, before you add the sugar.

Fromage frais makes great, edible glue.

Red liquorice makes good arms.

Funky junk flowers

You will need

★ small, low-sided cardboard cartons ★ coloured card ★ scissors
★ paint ★ wooden sticks or garden canes ★ glue ★ sticky tape
★ glitter, pom-poms, fabric scraps to decorate

What to do

1 Paint the cardboard cartons in bright colours to make the flower centres. Cut out petal and leaf shapes from coloured card. They must be large enough to show around the flower centres.

2 Glue the petals and then the leaves to the back of the cartons. Decorate your flowers any way you like, with glitter, pom-poms, pipe cleaners, or fabric scraps.

3 Attach the flowers to their stems using glue or sticky tape. We used garden canes, but any stick would do.

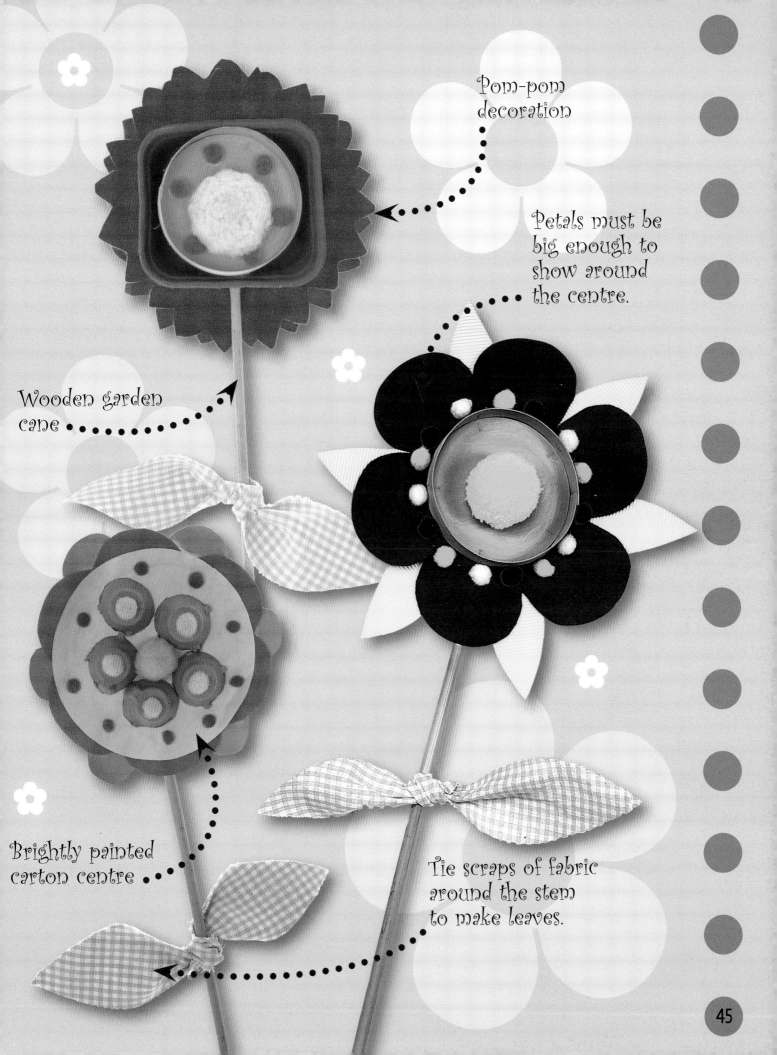

Pom-pom
decoration

Petals must be
big enough to
show around
the centre.

Wooden garden
cane

Brightly painted
carton centre

Tie scraps of fabric
around the stem
to make leaves.

45

Wacky scarecrow

You will need

★ 2 thick poles or sticks, one slightly longer than the other

★ string ★ straw ★ large piece of sackcloth ★ hat ★ scarf

★ old clothes, such as a shirt, trousers, jacket, rubber boots ★ gloves

What to do

1 Make a cross with two poles and tie them together with string. To make the head, lay out the large square of sackcloth and place a pile of straw in the middle. Draw up each of the corners and tie them together to make a ball. Tie the head to the pole.

2 Glue or paint on eyes and a mouth. A carrot makes a good nose. Cut a small cross in the sackcloth and push it in. A bright scarf and an old hat bring the scarecrow to life.

3 Put the shirt over the frame and tie string around the cuffs. Stuff it with straw. Tie the trouser legs and stuff them. Attach them to the top part of the body by looping string over the shoulders. Put on the jacket and boots.

Cut holes in the hat
and stuff with straw.

A bright scarf
hides where the head
joins the body.

Cut waterproof eyes
and a mouth out of a
white plastic bag.

Fix a long length of
string to the gloves and
thread them through
the jacket arms.

Stick the pole
into the ground.

Rubber boots

Templates

Trace the outline of the template you need onto tracing paper and cut it out. Place it on your coloured card, draw around it, then cut out your shape.

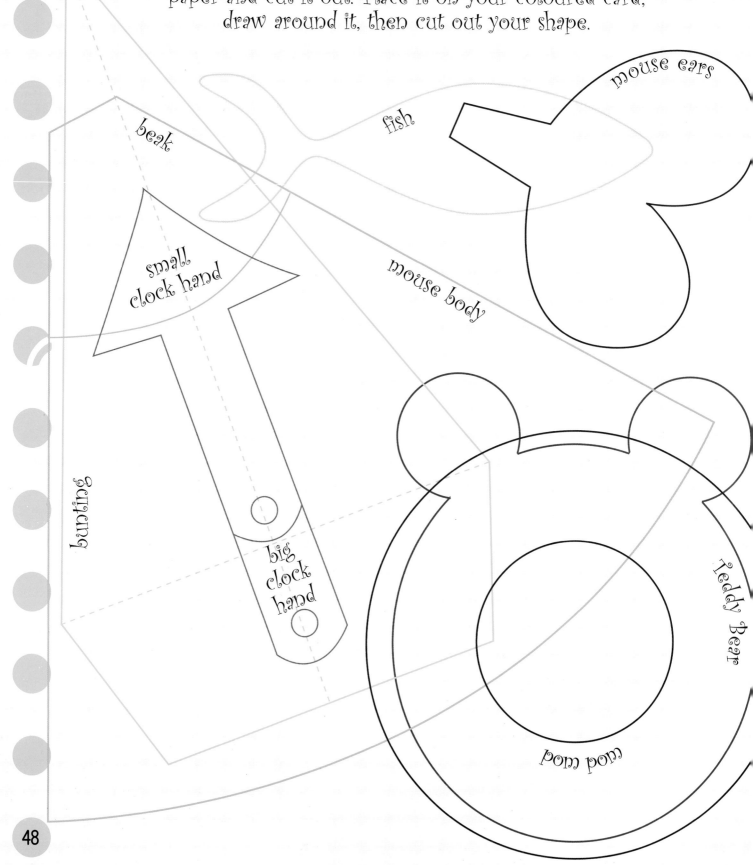

mouse ears

fish

beak

small
clock hand

mouse body

bunting

big
clock
hand

Teddy Bear

pom pom